World Wisdom
The Library of Perennial Philosophy

The Library of Perennial Philosophy is dedicated to the exposition of the timeless Truth underlying the diverse religions. This Truth, often referred to as the *Sophia Perennis*—or Perennial Wisdom—finds its expression in the revealed Scriptures as well as the writings of the great sages and the artistic creations of the traditional worlds.

The Perennial Philosophy provides the intellectual principles capable of explaining both the formal contradictions and the underlying unity of the great religions.

Ranging from the writings of the great sages who have expressed the *Sophia Perennis* in the past, to the perennialist authors of our time, each series of our Library has a different focus. As a whole, they express the inner unanimity, transforming radiance, and irreplaceable values of the great spiritual traditions. *The Sermon of All Creation: Christians on Nature* appears as one of our selections in the Sacred Worlds series.

Sacred Worlds Series

The Sacred Worlds series blends images of visual beauty with focused selections from the writings of the great religions of the world, including both Scripture and the writings of the sages and saints. Books in the Sacred Worlds series may be based upon a particular religious tradition, or a theme of interest, such as prayer and virtue, which are found in all manifestations of the sacred.

The Sermon of All Creation

Christians on Nature

Edited by

Judith Fitzgerald
and
Michael Oren Fitzgerald

Foreword by John Chryssavgis

World Wisdom

www.worldwisdom.com

The Sermon of All Creation: Christians on Nature
©2005 World Wisdom, Inc.

Design by Judith Fitzgerald

Library of Congress Cataloging-in-Publication Data

The sermon of all creation: Christians on nature / edited by Judith Fitzgerald and Michael
Oren Fitzgerald ; foreword by John Chryssavgis.
     p. cm. – (Sacred worlds series)
  Includes bibliographical references and index.
  ISBN 0-941532-78-X (pbk. : alk. paper)
  1. Nature– -Religious aspects– –Christianity- -History of doctrines. I. Fitzgerald, Judith, 1951-
II. Fitzgerald, Michael Oren, 1949- III. Sacred worlds series (Bloomington, Ind.)
  BT695 .5 .S47 2005
  231. 7- -dc22

2004025693

Printed on acid-free paper in China.

For information address World Wisdom, Inc.
P.O. Box 2682, Bloomington, Indiana 47402-2682

Table of Contents

FOREWORD

It may be tempting, though surely misleading, to imagine the current environmental crisis as a recent phenomenon. Human beings have from the outset ignored the "voice" of creation, selfishly shutting themselves off from the breadth and depth of the mystery of the universe that declares the wonder of God. Such is perhaps the root of our original sin: not a transgression against some invisible "principle," but the rupture of the primal connection between ourselves, our world, and our God. How unfortunate it is that we have reduced the concept of sin to individual guilt, while overlooking the social and cosmological implications of sin, whereby division and brokenness are introduced into the world, barring us from discerning God in all things and all things in God.

It may be equally convenient, though clearly incorrect, to believe that the contemporary response to the environmental crisis is historically unprecedented. Those who received inspiration from the holiness of the uncreated Divine have always perceived insights into the wholeness of the created cosmos. Across traditions and cultures, these sages have both recognized and reflected on the harmony of heaven and earth, struggling—albeit imperfectly and incompletely—to retain the connections between a flower in the fields, a ray of sunlight, and the glory of God. That is how they understood the sense of beauty. And that is how they appreciated the concept of sin. For they were convinced that the way we treat the animal and material environment mirrored the worship and honor that we reserved for God.

✝✝✝

The Christian sages, men and women, whose voice is captured in this anthology, are derived from East and West. They comprise writers of old and of recent times. They are saints and sinners alike. They range from writers of the Old Testament to books of the New Testament; from Augustine of Hippo to Gregory of Nyssa, and from Hildegard of Bingen to Therese of Lisieux; from Martin Luther to John Calvin, and from Ralph Waldo Emerson to Henry David Thoreau. Their words are supposed to be read slowly; their intention is to take the reader by the hand and lead them outside: to the beauty of creation. This beauty is there for us to behold; it is also there for us to hold onto dearly. Ultimately, of course, the purpose is to draw together the outside and the inside, the visible and the invisible, the universe and the heart, where the perennial beauty of God lies.

Yet, there is indeed something unique about our age inasmuch as, perhaps for the first time in human history, we are in a position to choose the direction of our world. Based on knowledge achieved and experience gained, we are able to embrace attitudes and espouse choices that will immediately affect and impact our world as well as the world that our children will inherit. The decisions and actions of former generations and eras were, at least to a degree, determined by nature or by culture. Today, however, we have the information at hand; science has alerted us to the devastating consequences of our extravagant and wasteful lifestyles in so-called Western countries. If only we could look beyond ourselves, we might just approach some resolution. If only we would turn outside ourselves—to other human beings living in stark poverty and unacceptable conditions (even among us!), to other societies affected by our unequal and unfair consumption of the earth's resources, or to other geographical regions depleted by social and economic injustice or devastated by warfare. Then we might just anticipate a more personal response to the plight of our waters, of our forests, and of our planet.

Where we are personally challenged for change is where daily life translates into environmental ethics. It is where life, spirituality, and politics coincide. The voice of creation is eloquent and clear. The choice is ours.

John Chryssavgis

INTRODUCTION

This book collects Christian writings on the nature of creation from the time of the Bible through the 19th century. The resulting message constitutes an inspiring expression of our relationship with our Creator through the *wonders* of the natural world—a sermon of all creation.

The time period covered by these writings is limited to giants of the Christian faith who were born and wrote prior to the 20th century, thus before evidence of the growing environmental crisis was plain for all to see. As the industrial revolution gained momentum during the 20th century, with its ever-increasing appetite for devouring our natural resources, an environmental call to arms echoed with growing intensity. The environmental writings from the 20th and 21st century were penned, in varying degrees, from a compulsion to explain and to respond to this mounting desecration of the natural world. In contrast, the Christian writers from Biblical times through the 19th century wrote without the duress of looming environmental catastrophes; thus, their writings are solely based on an unbounded love and devotion for both the Creator and His creation. These sages represent all the major branches of Christianity; while some of them might disagree on other theological points, they are all of one mind concerning the essential Christian perspective on creation. Allowing for inevitable differences in emphasis, this collection of writings therefore represents the unity of the Christian tradition as regards the beauty and the majesty of the universe and man's place within that universe.

But the gift of creation requires an appropriate response from each person. The words of these spiritual seekers bear witness to their *knowledge* of the relationship between God and His creation, and to an unbounded *love* for both creation and the Creator. Their thoughts manifest an unsurpassed joy that will inspire others to follow their lofty example. But the Biblical passages concerning creation should also instill a certain *fear* in those who are not fulfilling the responsibilities established by the Creator. For instance, just after the Creator grants mankind "dominion … over all the earth,"[1] the Bible goes on to add, "And God said, 'Be fruitful and multiply, and *replenish the earth*, and subdue it.…'"[2] (emphasis added). We have collected the most applicable Biblical quotations setting forth the covenant God established with our ancestors regarding the natural world. As one example relates:

> If you walk in my statutes, and keep my commandments … then I will give you rain in due season, and the land shall yield her increase, and the trees of the field shall yield their fruit.… And I will have respect unto you, and make you fruitful … and establish my covenant with you.[3]

And another:

> So these things shall be for a statute of judgment unto you through-out your generations in all your dwellings. Whoso killeth any per-

---

[1] Genesis 1:26. All citations are from the King James version of the Bible.

[2] Genesis 1:28. During the 1970s and 1980s some secular environmentalists took certain Biblical phrases, such as "…and subdue it," out of context and strongly criticized Christianity as the only major world religion to be actively hostile toward the environment. Because this unjust criticism has been corrected by other works, we will merely note that religion is not the cause for the current environmental crisis, which only began when we increasingly lost sight of our religious teachings.

[3] Leviticus 26:3-9.

son, the murderer shall be put to death.... So you shall not pollute the land wherein you are.... Defile not therefore the land which ye shall inhabit, wherein I dwell.[4]

Our ability to exercise dominion over the earth must therefore be balanced by recognition of the corresponding responsibility placed upon all Christians, which is both collective and individual. Even if the time for society's worst environmental reckonings does not come during our lifetime, each of us must nevertheless account to the Creator for our actions when we leave this mortal life. Failure to accept our individual responsibility not to "pollute the land" and to "replenish the earth" will have its own consequences when each of us meets our Creator. A correct reading of the Biblical injunctions included in this collection should therefore send an urgent message to every Christian and to people of other faiths who recognize the Bible as a source of divinely-inspired wisdom.

During the past century the environmental call to arms has been answered by an exponential increase in writings by people of all faiths, and people without faith, who are outraged by the indifference of our society toward mounting ecological problems. The argumentation of most environmentalists is primarily secular, based largely on a growing body of scientific evidence that measures the impact of past pollution and forecasts the consequences of maintaining current industrial practices. While these arguments

[4] Numbers 35:29-30, 33-34. Regardless of one's opinions about capital punishment, it is notable that the admonition against polluting the earth is included in the same context as the proscription against murder.

are compelling in many respects, they have not been sufficient to awaken the majority of people from their somnolent attitude toward impending natural catastrophe, including the depletion of important natural resources. People appear to be asleep to these problems because they do not want to deal with the inevitable consequences of the solutions.

A meaningful change in the world's environmental trajectory will entail a reevaluation of many aspects of our present way of life, which is built upon an excessive materialism and consumerism. Private industry has failed to lead the way toward adequate solutions; rather, it attempts to increase the pace of consumerism. The outward difficulties resulting from a change in lifestyle will inevitably cause emotional pain for anyone who is focused on achieving a maximum of material comfort at the lowest cost. It is easier to deny the growing evidence of environmental damage and postpone the major reckonings to future generations. In a world dominated by democracy, governmentally mandated change in environmental policies will not occur until a plurality is willing to stand shoulder to shoulder with our leaders and accept the outward difficulties and emotional pain that will result.

What are the ways to build the necessary resolve for this change? Resolve must be built upon understanding—in this case the understanding that the current environmental crisis stems from an underlying spiritual crisis. For the most part, Christians in the modern world have retired from the environmental debate and allowed science to define the universe and set our expectations. Many of the roots of this "age of science" can be traced back to the Renaissance, when a quest for a rational explanation of the physical world began to replace the long-standing spiritual traditions that placed more reliance on the spiritual and metaphysical explanations of our place in the cosmos. Prior to this time our "faith" was firmly placed in spiritual truths that explained our role and responsibilities in relationship to God and to creation. In the search for purely measurable explanations, scientific methodology became more important than spiritual truth.

Scientism is based upon the assumption that rational thought and experimental methods are the means of human knowledge, and that the key to society's well-being is the quantifiable understanding of our material universe. Based upon the technological marvels that have resulted from such methods and measurements, we have been led to believe in the idea of a perpetual "progress" through continually improving material comforts and expanding opportunities for individual empowerment. Thus, in many respects, our "faith" has changed from being focused on the spiritual domain to being focused on the scientific domain. While scientism has produced many important inventions and has developed various theories about how the cosmos was created, no scientific method or measurement can explain the most basic question: what is the meaning of life?

There is an ongoing debate about the timetable for various environmental reckonings that includes questions such as the ability of the planet to renew itself and the ability of science to find a panacea.[5] But there can be no doubt that the earth is already in trouble and if we maintain our current trajectory there will eventually be a series of natural catastrophes. We may conclude that an environmentalism that is over-reliant upon science and the myth of perpetual progress will fail to avert those catastrophes.

---

[5] A core theory of scientism is that there is no absolute answer to any question; thus every answer is provisional and relative. It follows that we must continually challenge every measurement and assumption to find alternative answers, leading to a never-ending debate.

spiritual imperative not to "pollute the land" and to "replenish the earth."

    This collection of inspired writings is not a systematic or exhaustive treatise on the Christian perspective toward creation; nor is it a complete explanation of how and why we have forgotten our spiritual responsibility toward creation. *The Sermon of All Creation* is intended to provide keys for Christians of every denomination— as well as spiritual seekers of all faiths—to build the necessary resolve to protect the treasures of our natural world. The resolve starts with individuals, then reaches to their neighbors, and finally spreads throughout large segments of society. But resolve must come firstly from the *knowledge* that the environmental crisis is at root a spiritual crisis; secondly, from the *love* in our hearts for the Creator, who has given us both the miracle of life and the wonders of the world that surround us; and, thirdly, from the *fear* of violating the covenant that God has established with us. When we begin to focus on spiritual principles, there will be no emotional pain as we welcome the changes in lifestyle necessary to stop the desecration of nature. We pray that this sermon of all creation will help bring about this change of heart.

Judith and Michael Fitzgerald
Bloomington, Indiana
November, 2004

Creation is a great book. Look above you; look below you! Note it; read it! God didn't write that book with ink. Instead, He set before your eyes the things that He had made. Can you ask for a louder voice than that? Why, heaven and earth cry out to you, "God made me!"

Augustine of Hippo (354-430)

*W*hen I consider thy heavens, the work of thy fingers, the moon and the stars, which thou hast ordained, what is man, that thou art mindful of him?

Psalm 8:3-4

*B*elief in God rests on the art and wisdom displayed in the order of the world: the belief in the Unity of God, on the perfection that must belong to Him in respect of power, goodness, wisdom, etc.

Gregory of Nyssa (330-395)

*L*isten to the sermon preached to you by the flowers, the trees, the shrubs, the sky, and the whole world. Notice how they preach to you a sermon full of love, of praise of God, and how they invite you to glorify the sublimity of that sovereign Artist who has given them being.

Paul of the Cross (1694-1775)

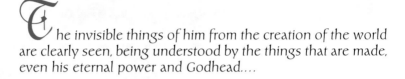

he invisible things of him from the creation of the world are clearly seen, being understood by the things that are made, even his eternal power and Godhead....

Romans 1:20

an is not a being isolated from the rest of creation. By his very nature, he is bound up with the whole of the universe.... In his way to union with God, man in no way leaves creatures aside, but gathers together in his love the whole cosmos disordered by sin, that it may be transfigured by grace.

Maximus the Confessor (580-662)

othing can be got out of a thing which is not in it. Therefore every species, every genus, every natural order, is naturally developed within its own limits, bearing fruit after its own kind, and not within some other essentially different order: everything in which seed is sown must correspond to its own seed.

Richard the Englishman (ca. 16th/17th century)

reatures do not obviously interfere with our seeing of God. Nothing is at the same time both a support and an obstacle, and creatures, carrying in themselves as they do the trace and image of God, help us toward the knowledge of God.

Albert the Great (1193-1280)

e magnifies the Lord who observes with a keen understanding and most profound contemplation the greatness of creation, so that from the greatness and beauty of creatures he may contemplate their Creator. The deeper one penetrates into the reasons for which things in existence were made and were governed, the more [that person] contemplates the magnificence of the Lord and, as far as it lies in him, magnifies the Lord.

Basil the Great (329-379)

To the body and the mind which have been cramped by noxious work or company, nature is medicinal and restores their tone.

Ralph Waldo Emerson (1803-1882)

The whole wilderness seems to be alive and familiar, full of humanity. The very stones seem talkative, sympathetic, brotherly. No wonder when we consider that we all have the same Father and Mother.

Nature is ever at work building and pulling down, creating and destroying, keeping everything whirling and flowing, allowing no rest but in rhythmical motion, chasing everything in endless song out of one beautiful form into another.

In this beautiful work, every boulder is prepared and measured and put in its place more thoughtfully than are the stones of temples. If for a moment you are inclined to regard these talus slopes as mere draggled, chaotic dumps, climb to the top of one of them, tie your mountain shoes firmly over the instep, and with braced nerves run down without any haggling, puttering hesitation, boldly jumping from boulder to boulder with even speed. You will then find your feet playing a tune, and quickly discover the music and poetry of rock piles—a fine lesson; and all Nature's wilderness tells the same story. Storms of every sort, torrents, earthquakes, cataclysms, "convulsions of nature," etc., are only harmonious notes in the song of creation, varied expressions of God's love.

John Muir (1838-1914)

*T*wo great reservoirs of knowledge are available to man, the book of creatures and the book of Scriptures... Of the two books which have been given to him, man has possessed the book of nature from the beginning.

Ramon Sibiude (ca. 1378-1438)

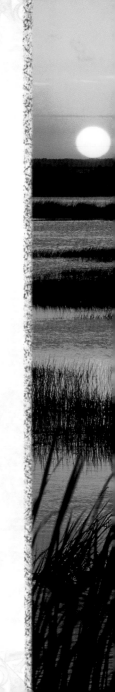

*T*he continuous shining of the sun is required for the preservation of light in the air; similarly God must confer existence on all things if they are to persevere in existence.... Therefore, God must be in all things.

Thomas Aquinas (ca. 1225-1274)

*E*vils abound in the world in order that the world may not engage our love. But what is this evil in the world? For the sky and the earth and the waters and the things that are in them, the fishes and the birds and the trees are not evil. All these are good. It is the actions of men who make the world evil.

Augustine of Hippo (354-430)

*F*or He produced things into being in order that His goodness might be communicated to them; and because His goodness could not be adequately represented by one creature alone, He produced many and diverse creatures, that what was wanting in one representation of the Divine Goodness might be supplied by another. For goodness, which in God is simple and uniform, in creatures is manifold and divided; and hence the whole universe together participates in the Divine Goodness more perfectly, and represents it better than any single creature whatever.

Thomas Aquinas (ca. 1225-1274)

The divine activity permeates the whole universe. It pervades every creature. Wherever they are, it is there. He moves about the smallest blades of grass as well as above the mighty cedar. The grains of sand are under His feet as well as the huge mountains. Wherever you may turn, there you will find His footprints!

Jean-Pierre de Caussade (1675-1751)

God creates everything, but He remains uncreated. The fact that the world has a beginning is confirmed by nature and taught us by history.... Creation is not from God's essence; it is not the uncreated energies of God, but the result of the uncreated energies....To "beget" is the property of God's nature, but to "create" is the property of His energy and will. If there were no distinction between essence and energies, between nature and will, then the creatures would belong by nature to God....

Man is animal in his body, but his soul originated in the transcendental world (*hyperkosmion*) and is a superior creation. Man was made paradoxically a small world (*mikrokosmos*) in which is summarized all the rest of creation. For this reason He created man to stand between, to include and to beautify, both worlds, the visible and the invisible.

Gregory Palamas (1296-1359)

In this light my spirit suddenly saw through all, and in and by all the creatures, even in herbs and grass; it knew God, who He is and how He is and what His will is. And suddenly in that light my will was set on by a mighty impulse to describe the Being of God.

Jacob Boehme (1575-1624)

God is an artist, and the universe is His work of art.

Thomas Aquinas (ca. 1225-1274)

In the woods too, a man casts off his years, as the snake his slough, and at what period soever of life, is always a child. In the woods, is perpetual youth. Within these plantations of God, a decorum and sanctity reign, a perennial festival is dressed, and the guest sees not how he should tire of them in a thousand years. In the woods, we return to reason and faith. There I feel that nothing can befall me in life, — no disgrace, no calamity, (leaving me my eyes,) which nature cannot repair. Standing on the bare ground, — my head bathed by the blithe air, and uplifted into infinite space, — all mean egotism vanishes. I become a transparent eye-ball; I am nothing; I see all; the currents of the Universal Being circulate through me; I am part or particle of God.... In the wilderness, I find something more dear and connate than in streets or villages. In the tranquil landscape, and especially in the distant line of the horizon, man beholds somewhat as beautiful as his own nature.

Ralph Waldo Emerson (1803-1882)

*A*rt cannot change or overstep
the natural order or the universe.

Henry Madathanas (1575-1639)

*A*ll science has but one aim, namely, to find a theory of
nature. We have theories of races and of functions, but scarcely
yet a remote approach to an idea of creation. We are now so
far from the road to truth, that religious teachers dispute and
hate each other, and speculative men are esteemed unsound and
frivolous....Whenever a true theory appears, it will be its own
evidence. Its test is, that it will explain all phenomena.

Ralph Waldo Emerson (1803-1882)

*T*he concept of every single thing in the entire universe has
been with the eternal wisdom for all time. As the ages pass, God
allows these concepts and ideas to emerge. Now suppose that
you knew all the concepts which have nothing to do with you....
It is surely clear that we shall not assume that image which the
eternal wisdom wishes us to have by trying to understand all the
mysterious activities of God down through the centuries. We can
receive God's seal on our souls only by abandoning our will to
him, not by any efforts of our reason.

Jean-Pierre de Caussade (1675-1751)

f all the strengths of God's creation, man's is the most profound, made in a wondrous way with great glory from the dust of the earth, and so entangled with the strengths of the rest of creation that he can never be separated from them.

Hildegard of Bingen   (1098-1179)

*T*hese creatures minister to our needs every day: without them we could not live; and through them the human race greatly offends the Creator. We fail every day to appreciate so great a blessing by not praising as we should the Creator and Dispenser of all these gifts.

Francis of Assisi (1182-1226)

*C*onsider the infinite, multiple power of the seed—how many grasses, fruits and animals are contained in each kind of seed; and how there surges from each a beautiful, innumerable multiplicity of forms. Contemplate with your inner eye how in a master the many laws of an art or science are one; how they live in a spirit that disposes them. Contemplate how an infinite number of lines may cross through a single point, and other similar examples drawn from nature.

From the contemplation of such examples as these, raised above all things by the wings of natural contemplation, illumined and supported by divine grace, you will be able to penetrate by the keenness of your mind the secrets of the Word and, to the extent that it is granted to the human being who seeks signs of his God, you will see how all things made by the Word live in the Word and are life: "For in Him," as the sacred Scripture says, "we live and move and have our being."

John Scotus Eriugena (810-877)

It is evident that if a man practices a compassionate affection for animals, he is all the more disposed to feel compassion for his fellow men.

Thomas Aquinas (ca. 1225-1274)

Throughout the entire creation, the manifest wisdom of God shines forth from Him and in Him, as in a mirror containing the beauty of all forms and lights and as in a book in which all things are written according to the deep secrets of God. O, if only I could find this book whose origin is eternal, whose essence is incorruptible, whose knowledge is life, whose script is indelible, whose study is desirable, whose teaching is easy, whose knowledge is sweet, whose depth is inscrutable, whose words are ineffable, yet all are a single Word! Truly, whoever finds this book will find life and will draw salvation from the Lord.

Bonaventure (1217-1274)

The day of my spiritual awakening was the day I saw, and knew I saw, all things in God and God in all things.

Mechthild of Magdeburg
(1210-1297)

The little birds singing are singing of God; the beasts cry unto Him; the elements are in awe of Him; the mountains echo His name; the waves and streams cast their glances at Him; the herbs and flowers praise Him. Nor do we need to labor or seek Him far off, since each one of us finds (God) within himself, inasmuch as we are all upheld and preserved by His power dwelling in us.

John Calvin (1509-1564)

The seed of God is in us. Given an intelligent farmer and a diligent fieldhand, it will thrive and grow up to God whose seed it is and, accordingly, its fruit will be God-nature. Pear seeds grow into pear trees, nut seeds into nut trees, and God-seed into God.

Meister Eckhart (1260-1327)

This doctrine from the book of nature opens up to all a way of understanding the holy Doctors (of the Church); indeed, it is incorporated in their books (even though it is not always evident in them) as an alphabet is incorporated in all writings. For it is the alphabet of the Doctors: as such it should be learned first. For which reason, to make your way towards the Holy Scriptures you will do well to acquire this science as the rudiments of all sciences; in order the better to reach conclusions, learn it before everything else, otherwise you will hardly manage to struggle through to the … higher sciences: for this is the root, the origin and the tiny foundation of the doctrine proper to Man and His salvation….

And there is no need that anyone should refrain from reading it [the book of nature] from lack of other learning: it presupposes no knowledge of Grammar, Logic, nor any other deliberative art or science, nor Physics nor of Metaphysics, seeing that it is the doctrine which comes first….This doctrine is common to the laity, the clergy and all manner of people: yet it can be grasped in less than a month, and without learning anything by heart. No books are required, for once it has been perceived, it cannot be forgotten….It uses no obscure arguments requiring lengthy discourse: for it argues from things which are evident and known to all from experience—from the creatures and the nature of Man; from what he knows of himself, it proves what it seeks to prove, mainly from what each man has assayed of himself. And there is no need of any other witness but Man.

Ramon Sibiude (ca. 1378-1438)

od is substantially present everywhere, in and through all creatures, in all their parts and places, so that the world is full of God and He fills all, but without His being encompassed and surrounded by it. He is at the same time outside and above all creatures. These are all exceedingly incomprehensible matters; yet they are articles of our faith and are attended clearly and mightily in Holy Writ.... For how can reason tolerate it that the divine majesty is so small that it can be substantially present in a grain, on a grain, over a grain, through a grain, within and without, and that, although it is a single Majesty, it nevertheless is entirely in each grain separately, no matter how immeasurably numerous these grains may be? ... And that the same Majesty is so large that neither this world nor a thousand worlds can encompass it and say: "Behold, there it is!" His one divine Essence can be in all creatures collectively and in each one individually more profoundly, more immanently, more present, than the creature is in itself; yet it can be encompassed nowhere and by no one. It encompasses all things and dwells in all, but not one thing encompasses it and dwells in it.

Martin Luther (1483-1546)

If God is to create or to preserve a creature, God must be present and must make and preserve God's creation both in its innermost and outermost aspects.... God's entire divine nature is wholly and entirely in all creatures, more deeply, more inwardly, more present than the creature is to itself.

Martin Luther (1483-1546)

If you were to look at every creature from the beginning of creation to the end of time, whether it were the most radiant angel or the tiniest worm, you would see in it signs of God's goodness and His overflowing love.

Aelred of Rievaulx (1110-1167)

If you want to understand the Creator, seek to understand created things.

Columba of Iona (521-597)

The highest Good, who himself alone doth please, made man good and for goodness, and gave this place to him as an earnest of eternal peace.

Dante (1265-1321)

See how the divine order embraces and extends to the smallest objects. A fish does not resist God's law, yet we men cannot endure His precepts of salvation! Do not despise fish because they are unreasoning; rather fear lest, in your resistance to the disposition of the Creator, you have even less reason than they. Listen to the fish, who by their actions all but speak and say: it is for the perpetuation of our species that we undertake this long voyage. They have not the gift of reason, but they have the law of nature firmly seated within them, to show what they have to do.

Basil the Great (329-379)

Creation is the accuser of the ungodly. For through its inherent spiritual principles, creation proclaims its Maker; and through the natural laws intrinsic to each individual species it instructs us in virtue. The spiritual principles may be recognized in the unremitting continuance of each individual species, the laws in the consistency of its natural activity. If we do not ponder on these things, we remain ignorant of the cause of created being and we cling to all the passions which are contrary to nature.

Maximus the Confessor (580-662)

How late I came to love you, O Beauty so ancient and so fresh, how late I came to love you! You were within me, yet I had gone outside to seek you. Unlovely myself, I rushed toward all those lovely things you had made. And always you were with me, I was not with you. All these beauties kept me far from you—although they would not have existed at all unless they had their being in you. You called, you cried, you shattered my deafness. You sparkled, you blazed, you drove away my blindness. You shed your fragrance, and I drew in my breath and I panted for you. I tasted and now I hunger and thirst. You touched me, and now I burn with longing for your peace.

Augustine of Hippo (354-430)

This world, with all its stars, elements, and creatures, is come out of the invisible world; it has not the smallest thing or the smallest quality of anything but what is come forth from thence.

William Law (1613-1673)

*T*he plants give off the fragrance of their flowers. The precious stones reflect their brilliance to others. Every creature yearns for a loving embrace. The whole of nature serves humanity, and in this service offers all her bounty.

Hildegard of Bingen (1098-1179)

*T*he humble man approaches wild animals, and the moment they catch sight of him their ferocity is tamed. They come up and cling to him as to their Master, wagging their tails and licking his hands and feet. They scent as coming from him the same fragrance that came from Adam before the transgression, the time when they were gathered together before him and he gave them names in Paradise. This scent was taken away from us, but Christ has renewed it and given it back to us at His coming. It is this which has sweetened the fragrance of humanity. Even the demons with their malice and fierceness, with the pride of their minds, become like dust once they have encountered a humble person.

Isaac the Syrian (7th century)

The happiest man is he who learns from nature the lesson of worship.

Ralph Waldo Emerson (1803-1882)

If, instead of stopping short at the outward appearance which visible things present to the senses, you seek with your intellect to contemplate their inner essences, seeing them as images of spiritual realities or as the inward principles of sensible objects, you will be taught that nothing belonging to the visible world is unclean. For by nature all things were created good.

Maximus the Confessor (580-662)

The laws of nature are just, but terrible. There is no weak mercy in them. Cause and consequence are inseparable and inevitable. The elements have no forbearance. The fire burns, the water drowns, the air consumes, the earth buries. And perhaps it would be well for our race if the punishment of crimes against the laws of man were as inevitable as the punishment of crimes against the laws of nature…were man as unerring in his judgments as nature.

Henry Wadsworth Longfellow (1815-1894)

*F*rom the creation, learn to admire the Lord! And if any of the things which you see exceed your comprehension, and you are not able to find the reason for its existence, then for this reason, glorify the Creator that the wisdom of His works surpasses your own understanding.

John Chrysostom   (347-407)

I love everything—the sun and the world—and I, the sinful one, fear that it might be idleness on my part to look on the beauty of the fields covered with wild flowers. No. This is acceptable...because the beauty was created by the Lord....I want to go into the field where the golden corn is growing and where, from the forest, comes an aromatic smell.... Even from childhood, I loved the smell of sweet, blossoming wild cherry trees, the babbling brooks, the dawns and sunsets. What inexplicable contrition of heart I used to feel, then as now, when the sun is meeting the early spring morning as its first rays of light are sprinkled upon the earth. What joy is born then in the heart of man.... In the east there is Paradise; otherwise the hearts of people would not tremble with exaltation at the sight of the morning light and the rays of sunlight. Otherwise, the eyes would not look with joy at the clearing of the dawn; and the birds of heaven would not glorify the Lord during spring mornings, those mornings which I would still like to see in this life.

Athanasia Logacheva (1809-1875)

All living creatures are, so to speak, sparks from the radiation of God's brilliance, and these sparks emerge from God like the rays of the sun.

Hildegard of Bingen (1098-1179)

No one is so foolish as not to believe that the things of the physical world are subject to someone's government, providence, and disposition, seeing that they are regulated according to a certain order and time. Thus we see the sun, the moon, and the stars and other parts of the physical world all holding a certain course, which would not happen if they were the sport of chance. For that reason, a man would be a fool not to believe in God.

Thomas Aquinas (ca. 1225-1274)

"The heavens declare the glory of God." How then, tell me, do they declare it? Voice have they none; mouth they do not possess; tongue is not theirs! How then do they declare? By means of the spectacle itself! For when you see the beauty, the breadth, the height, the position, the form, the stability thereof during so long a period, hearing as it were a voice, and being instructed by the spectacle itself, thou admirest Him who created a body so fair and strange! The heavens may be silent, but the sight of them emits a voice that is louder than a trumpet's sound.

John Chrysostom (347-407)

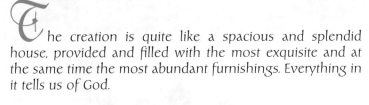

The creation is quite like a spacious and splendid house, provided and filled with the most exquisite and at the same time the most abundant furnishings. Everything in it tells us of God.

John Calvin (1509-1564)

Just as you see that a ray of light entering through a window is colored in different ways according to the different colors of the various parts, so the divine ray shines forth in each and every creature in different ways and in different properties.

Bonaventure (1217-1274)

There are things in creation hard to understand, or even undiscoverable for human beings. We are not in consequence to condemn the Creator of the universe just because we cannot discover the reason for the creation of scorpions or other venomous beasts. The right thing for a man who is aware of the weakness of our race and who knows it is impossible to understand the reasons of God's design even when most minutely examined, is to ascribe the knowledge of these things to God, who will later on, if we are judged worthy, reveal to us the matters about which we are now reverently in doubt.

Origen (185-254)

*L*et us not be ashamed to take pious delight in the works of God open and manifest in this beautiful theater....Wherever we cast our eyes, all things they meet are works of God, and at the same time (we should) ponder with pious meditation to what end God created them.

John Calvin (1509-1564)

*A*nyone able to investigate these beautiful features of creation could find in them the marvelous light of the wisdom of God. Would that I could as subtly see them and as competently tell of them as I am able ardently to love them. For I am delighted because it is very sweet and pleasant frequently to deal with these topics in which the senses are educated by reason and love is roused by emulation.

Hugh of St. Victor (1096-1141)

*M*ost men, it seems to me, do not care for nature and would sell their share in all her beauty, as long as they may live, for a stated sum, and many for a glass of rum. It is for the very reason that some do not care for those things that we need to continue to protect all from the vandalism of a few.

Henry David Thoreau (1817-1862)

The clearest way into the universe is through a forest wilderness.

John Muir (1838-1914)

Man was introduced last among exis-
tent things, as a natural bond between the ex-
tremes of the whole through his own parts, and
bringing into unity in his own person those
things which by nature are far distinct from
each other. Drawing all things out of their former division and bringing them united to God
by means available in the right sequence and
order, he finally reaches the goal of the sublime
ascent which is achieved through the union of
all things, attaining God in whom there is no
division. First, through his utterly dispassionate relationship to divine virtue he frees the
whole of nature from the attributes of male and
female.... Next by uniting paradise with the in-
habited land through holiness of life, he makes
a single earth, not divided into different parts,
but rather brought together, since he is not
dominated by any passionate attraction toward
any of its parts.

Maximus the Confessor (580-662)

God hears above
All hollow noise
The echo of his praise
In every creature's voice.

Angelus Silesius (1624-167

All that is sweet, delightful, and amiable in this world, in the serenity of the air, the fineness of seasons, the joy of light, the melody of sounds, the beauty of colors, the fragrancy of smells, the splendor of precious stones, is nothing else but Heaven breaking through the veil of this world, manifesting itself in such a degree and darting forth in such variety so much of its own nature.

William Law (1686-1761)

The Holy Word of the Father then, almighty and perfect, uniting with the universe and having everywhere unfolded His own powers, and having illumined all, both things seen and things invisible, holds them together and binds them to Himself, having left nothing void of His power, but on the contrary He quickens and sustains all things everywhere, each severally and all collectively; while He mingles in one the principles of all sensible existence, heat namely and cold, and wet and dry, and causes them not to conflict, but to make up one concordant harmony....

Obeying Him, even God the Word, things on earth have life and things in heaven have their order, for there is nothing that is and that takes place, but it has been made and stands by Him and through Him.

Athanasius (297-373)

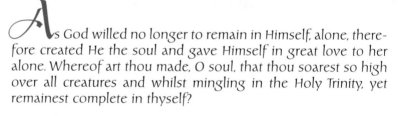

*A*s God willed no longer to remain in Himself, alone, therefore created He the soul and gave Himself in great love to her alone. Whereof art thou made, O soul, that thou soarest so high over all creatures and whilst mingling in the Holy Trinity, yet remainest complete in thyself?

Mechthild of Magdeburg (1210-1297)

*A*ll things that grow and sustain animal life He produced.... He gave us the earth, the fertility of soil, and food for men and animals....The truth is that all of these actions and energies belong to one true God, who is wholly present everywhere, is confined to no frontiers and bound by no hindrances, is indivisible and immutable, and though His nature has no need of either heaven or of earth, He fills them both with His presence and His power.

Augustine of Hippo (354-430)

*G*od wanted man to know him somehow through his creatures, and since no creature could fittingly reflect the infinite perfection of the Creator, he multiplied his creatures and gave a certain goodness and perfection to each of them so that from them we could judge the goodness and perfection of the Creator, who embraces infinite perfection in the perfection of his one and utterly simple essence.

Robert Bellarmine (1542-1621)

*f*or the word of God is quick, and powerful, and sharper than any two-edged sword, piercing even to the dividing asunder of soul and spirit, and of the joints and marrow, and is a discerner of the thoughts and intents of the heart. Neither is there any creature that is not manifest in His sight: but all things are naked and opened unto the eyes of Him with whom we have to do.

Hebrews 4:12-13

*f*or what purposes does He go up into the mountain? To teach us that loneliness and retirement is good when we are to pray to God. With this view, you see, He is continually withdrawing into the wilderness, and there often spends the whole night in prayer, teaching us earnestly to seek such quiet in our prayers, as the time and place may confer. For the wilderness is the mother of quiet; it is a calm and a harbor, delivering us from all turmoil.

John Chrysostom (347-407)

Ꮐod is in the universe and the universe is within God....Thus all things participate in God's sustaining energy, but not in His essence.

God, who fills all things and extends infinitely beyond the heavens, existed before the world, filling as He now fills the whole region of the world.

Gregory Palamas (1296-1359)

or God has not brought forth the creation, that he should be thereby perfect, but for his own manifestation, namely for the great joy and glory; not that this joy first began with the creation, no, for it was from eternity in the great mystery, yet only as a spiritual melody and sport in itself. The creation is the same sport out of himself, which he melodizes: and it is even as a great harmony of manifold instruments which are all tuned into one harmony.

Jacob Boehme (1575-1624)

his thou seest also in all God's works, how love hath poured itself into all things and is the most inward and out-ward foundation of all things....That, O God, is Thy inward spiritual kingdom as Thou dwellest in that which is hidden and fillest all Thy creatures and workest Thyself and doest all in all....

The true heaven is everywhere in this present time until the last day, and the house of wrath, of hell and death, is also in this world, now, everywhere, until the last day....Then will the earth, too, become crystalline, and the divine light will shine in all beings.

Jacob Boehme (1575-1624)

*L*et us turn our eyes to the Father and Creator of the universe, and when we consider how precious and peerless are His gifts of peace, let us embrace them eagerly for ourselves. Let us contemplate His purposes in creation, and consider how free from all anger He is toward His creatures and the total absence of any friction that marks the ordering of His whole creation.

Clement of Rome (37-101)

*S*ince the perfection of blessedness consists in the knowledge of God, He has been pleased, in order that none might be excluded from the means of obtaining felicity, not only to deposit in our minds that seed of religion of which we already have spoken, but so to manifest His perfections in the whole structure of the universe, and daily place Himself in our view, that we cannot open our eyes without being compelled to behold Him. His essence, indeed, is incomprehensible, utterly transcending all human thought; but on each of His works His glory is engraven in characters so bright, so distinct, and so illustrious, that none, however dull and illiterate, can plead ignorance as their excuse....Hence the author of the Epistle to the Hebrews elegantly describes the visible worlds as images of the invisible (Hebrews 11:3), the elegant structure of the world serving us as a kind of mirror, in which we may behold God, though otherwise invisible....

John Calvin (1509-1564)

*T*he human soul has three powers, first, the power of nourishment and growth; second, that of imagination and instinct; third, that of intelligence and intellect. Plants share only in the first of these powers; animals share in the first and second only; and men share in all three.

Maximus the Confessor (580-662)

*E*verything we see in nature is manifested truth; only we are not able to recognize it as such, unless truth is manifest within ourselves.... Look at the flowers of the fields; each one has its own particular attributes. Nevertheless they do not wrangle and fight with each other. They do not quarrel about the possession of sunshine as is daily provided by the philosophers who are disputing about the attributes and the will of God, and who nevertheless do not know God, because they do not listen to the word of God within their souls.

Jacob Boehme (1575-1624)

God is closer to me than I am to myself: my being depends on God's being near me and present to me. So He is also in a stone or a log of wood, only they do not know…. So man is more blessed than a stone or a piece of wood because he is aware of God and knows how close God is to him. And I am more blessed, the more I realize this.

Meister Eckhart (1260-1327)

"He was in the world, and the world was made by Him" (John 1:10). Do not imagine that He was in the world in such a way as the earth is in the world…or the trees, cattle and men are in the world. He was not in the world in such a way. But how was He? As the master builder who governs what He has made. For He did not make it in the way a craftsman makes a chest. The chest which he makes is external to him; and when it is constructed, it has been situated in another place. And however nearby he is, he who is constructing it sits in another place and is external to that which he is constructing…. But God constructs while infused in the world. He constructs while situated everywhere. He does not withdraw from anywhere. He does not direct the structure which He constructs as someone on the outside. By the presence of His majesty, He makes what He makes; by His own presence He governs what He has made.

Augustine of Hippo (354-430)

God showed me in my palm a little thing round as a ball about the size of a hazelnut. I looked at it with the eye of my understanding and asked myself: "What is this thing?"

And I was answered: "It is everything that is created." I wondered how it could survive since it seemed so little it could suddenly disintegrate into nothing. The answer came: "It endures and ever will endure, because God loves it." And so everything has being because of God's love.

Julian of Norwich (1342-1423)

*A*nyone who truly knows creatures may be excused from listening to sermons for every creature is full of God, and is a book.

Meister Eckhart (1260-1327)

*I*n every part of the world, in heaven and on earth, He has written and as it were engraven the glory of His power, goodness and eternity.... For all creatures, from the firmament even to the center of the earth, could be witnesses and messengers of His glory to all men, drawing them on to seek Him and, having found Him, to do Him service and honor according to the dignity of a Lord so good, so potent, so wise and everlasting.... For the little singing birds sang of God, the animals acclaimed Him, the elements feared and the mountains resounded with Him, the river and springs threw glances toward Him, the grasses and the flowers smiled.

John Calvin (1509-1564)

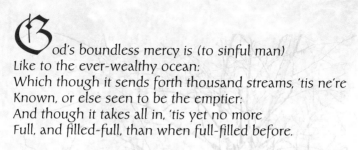

God's boundless mercy is (to sinful man)
Like to the ever-wealthy ocean:
Which though it sends forth thousand streams, 'tis ne're
Known, or else seen to be the emptier:
And though it takes all in, 'tis yet no more
Full, and filled-full, than when full-filled before.

Robert Herrick (1591-1674)

For this I thank You,
That You have created me in your image;
And You have placed your wonders under my hands,
So that I may know them and rejoice in your Creation.

I pray to You, Eternal God,
Give me your understanding and wisdom,
That I might not misuse your creation,
But make use of it only for my needs,
And for the good of my neighbor, myself and my family.

Give me gratitude for your gifts, so that my mind does not say,
"This is mine, I have bought it. I alone will possess it.
I am noble with it, majestic and beautiful;
It belongs to me because of my honor and glory."
All this comes from the devil and the grievous fall of Adam.

Jacob Boehme (1575-1624)

No single creature can express in full manner the likeness of God: it cannot be equal to God. The presence of multiplicity and variety among created things was therefore necessary that a perfect likeness to God be found in them according to their manner of being.

Albert the Great (1193-1280)

God is within all, over all, under all, is both above with His power and beneath with His support, exterior in respect to magnitude and interior in respect to subtlety, extending from the heights to the depths, encompassing the outside and penetrating the inside; but He is not in one part above, in another beneath, nor in one part exterior and in another interior. Rather, one and the same wholly and everywhere, He supports in presiding and presides in supporting, penetrates in encompassing and encompasses in penetrating.

Gregory the Great (540-604)

If your speech is full of wisdom and you meditate on understanding in your heart (cf. Psalm 49:3), you will discover in created things the presence of the divine Logos, the substantive Wisdom of God the Father (cf. 1 Corinthians 1:24); for in created things you will perceive the outward expression of the archetypes that characterize them, and thus through your active living intelligence, you will speak wisdom that derives from the Divine Wisdom.

Gregory of Sinai (1265-1346)

The universe too is one, not split between its visible and invisible parts, on the contrary. But the force of their reference to its own unity and indivisibility, circumscribes their differences in character. It shows itself to be the same, in the visible and invisible mutually joined without confusion with each other. Each is wholly fixed in the whole of the other. As parts of the whole, both make up the world, and as parts in the whole, both are completed and fulfilled in a single form. For the whole intelligible world of thought is visible to those who have eyes to see, spiritually expressed in symbolic form by the whole sensible universe. And the sensible world is mentally present in the whole intelligible universe when it is verbally expressed in the mind. For this visible world is verbally present in the world of thought; the world of thought is present in its visible images. Their end result or work is all one, "as it were a wheel in the middle of a wheel," says Ezekiel (1:16), that wonderful spectator of wonders, speaking, I think, about these two worlds. And the divine Apostle says," The invisible things of him from the creation of the world are clearly seen, being understood by the things that are made" (Romans 1:20).

If visible things can be observed through sense data, as it is written, visible phenomena will often be understood spiritually through the medium of what is sensibly imperceptible, by persons who devote themselves to spiritual contemplation. The contemplation of objects of thought symbolized through the objects of sight means the spiritual understanding of the seen through the unseen. Things which are significative of each other are bound to contain clear and perfectly true expressions of each other, and a flawless relation to them.

Maximus the Confessor (580-662)

*T*he initial step for a soul to come to knowledge of God is contemplation of nature.

Irenaeus of Lyons (129-203)

*I*t is possible to understand by every tree the knowledge of the divine power derived from created things. In the words of the divine apostle, "The invisible things of Him from the creation of the world are clearly seen, being understood by the things that are made" (Romans 1:20).

John Damascene (675-749)

*T*he trees of the Lord are full of sap; the cedars of Lebanon, which he hath planted; where the birds make their nests: as for the stork, the fir trees are her house. The high hills are a refuge for the wild goats; and the rocks for the conies. He appointed the moon for seasons: the sun knoweth his going down.... O Lord, how manifold are thy works! In wisdom hast thou made them all: the earth is full of thy riches.

Psalm 104:16-19, 24

*f*rom the supreme God, whose beauty is unseen and ineffable, Providence reaches down even to these earthly things below: all of which things, so transitory and momentary, could not have their peculiar, richly assorted beauties, but from that intellectual and immutable Beauty forming them all.

Augustine of Hippo (354-430)

The power of God is present at all places, even in the tiniest leaf.... God is entirely and personally present in the wilderness, in the garden, and in the field.

Martin Luther (1483-1546)

And he said, Whereunto shall we liken the kingdom of God? Or with what comparison shall we compare it? It is like a grain of mustard seed, which, when it is sown in the earth, is less than all the seeds that be in the earth: But when it is sown, it groweth up, and becometh greater than all herbs, and shooteth out great branches; so that the fowls of the air may lodge under the shadow of it.

Mark 4:30-32

We ought not to understand God and the creatures as two things distinct from one another, but as one and the same. For both the creature, by subsisting, is in God; and God, by manifesting himself, in a marvelous and ineffable manner, creates himself in creatures.

John Scotus Eriugena (810-877)

It is God's custom to care for all of His creatures, both the greatest and the least. We should likewise care for the creatures, whatsoever they are, in the sense that we use them in conformity with the divine purpose, in order that they may not bear witness against us in the Day of Judgment.

Thomas Aquinas (ca. 1225-1274)

My discussion has left out many things, and especially left out things incorporeal and invisible, that you may abhor those who blaspheme the wise and good Artificer, and from what is spoken and read, and whatever you can discover or conceive, from the greatness and beauty of the creatures, you may proportionately see the Maker of them. And bending the knee with godly reverence to the Maker of the worlds, the worlds of sense and thought, both visible and invisible, you may with a single and holy tongue, with unwearied lips and heart, praise God, and say how wonderful are thy works, O Lord; in wisdom hast thou made them all.

Cyril of Jerusalem (315-386)

*N*ever will I forget the impression the sea made upon me; I couldn't take my eyes off it since its majesty, the roaring of its waves, everything spoke to my soul of God's grandeur and power.

Therese of Lisieux (1873-1897)

*T*he Sages have been taught of God that this natural world is only an image and material copy of a heavenly and spiritual pattern; that the very existence of this world is based upon the reality of its celestial archetype.

Michael Sendivogius (d. 1646)

*G*od is not only to be known in His blessed and incomprehensible being, for this is something which is reserved for His saints in the age to come. He is also to be known from the grandeur and beauty of His creatures, from His providence which governs the world day by day, from His righteousness and from the wonders which He shows to His saints in each generation.... When we consider that He numbers the raindrops, the sand of the sea and the stars of heaven, we are amazed at the grandeur of His nature and His wisdom.

John Cassian (ca. 360-435)

In the next world we shall have no need of the sun, for we shall see with divine vision, by the light of our own nature.

Jacob Boehme (1575-1624)

God of our ancestors, Lord of mercy, who by your word have made all things, and in your wisdom have fitted man to rule the creatures that have come from you, to govern the world in holiness and justice and in honesty of soul to wield authority, grant me Wisdom, consort of your throne, and do not reject me from the number of your children.

Wisdom of Solomon 9:1-4

The earth is the Lord's and the fullness thereof.
O God, enlarge within us the sense of fellowship with all living things, even our brothers, the animals, to whom Thou gavest the earth as their home in common with us.
We remember with shame that in the past we have exercised the high dominion of man with ruthless cruelty so that the voice of the earth, which should have gone up to thee in song, has been a groan of pain.
May we realize that they live, not for us alone, but for themselves and for Thee and that they love the sweetness of life.

Basil the Great (329-379)

The land shall not be sold for ever: for the land is mine, for ye are strangers and sojourners with me. And in all the land of your possession ye shall grant a redemption for the land.

Leviticus 25:23-24

See a golden chain, see the order of the precious links, see how in a beautiful circle the beginning is fastened to the end.

Peter Sterry (1613-1672)

Nature is school-mistress, the soul the pupil; and whatever one has taught or the other has learned has come from God—the Teacher of the teacher.

Tertullian (160-230)

Now God, though He is absolutely immaterial, can alone by His own power produce matter by creation; and so He alone can produce a form in matter, without the aid of any preceding material form....Therefore, as no pre-existing body had been formed, through whose power another body of the same species could be generated, the first human body was of necessity made immediately by God.

Thomas Aquinas (ca. 1225-1274)

aze at the sky, the earth, the sea, and all the things which shine in them or above them, or creep or fly or swim beneath them. They have forms because they have rhythm: take this away, and they will no longer be. From whom then are they, save from Him, from whom rhythm is; since they have being only in so far as they are rhythmically ordered....Pass, therefore, beyond the mind of the artist, so that thou mayest see the everlasting rhythm; then will wisdom shine upon thee from her inmost abode, from the very sanctuary of truth.

Augustine of Hippo (354-430)

he great architect of the universe conceived and produced a being endowed with both natures, the visible and the invisible. God created the human being, bringing its body forth from the pre-existing matter which He animated with His own Spirit.... Thus in some way a new universe was born, small and great at one and the same time.

God set this "hybrid" worshiper on earth to contemplate the visible world, and to be initiated into the invisible; to reign over earth's creatures, and to obey orders from on high. He created a being at once earthly and heavenly, insecure and immortal, visible and invisible, halfway between greatness and nothingness, flesh and spirit at the same time...an animal en route to another native land, and, most mysterious of all, made to resemble God by simple submission to the divine will.

Gregory Nazianzus (329-389)

Every creature under heaven serves and acknowledges and obeys its Creator in its own way.

Francis of Assisi (1182-1226)

Despite characteristics that produce conflict (the lion cannot be blamed for having characteristics harmful to the lamb) there is an order in their manner of living. In nature no one species, left to itself, will multiply to the point of dominance. The diversity and inequality of the creation are necessary for order, which means the orderly working together of many creatures differing among themselves in graduation of intellect, in form and in species.

The diversity and inequality in created things are not the result of chance, not of a diversity of matter, nor of the intervention of certain causes or merit, but of the intention of God Himself, who wills to give the creature such perfection as it is possible for it to have.

Thomas Aquinas (ca. 1225-1274)

W here the contemplative life is concerned, the night supplies us with many themes for contemplation. First of all, it reminds us of the creation of the world, since all creation becomes invisible because of the darkness, as it was before it came into existence. This in turn prompts us to reflect how the sky was empty then and without stars, as happens now when they become invisible because of the clouds. When we see only darkness, we are reminded of the darkness that was over the abyss, and when suddenly the sky becomes clear again [and day returns], we are struck by wonder at the world above, and offer praise to God, just as did the angels who are said to have praised God when they saw the stars.

Peter of Damascus (ca. 1027-1107)

I wish you could come here and rest a year in the simple un-mingled Love-fountains of God. You would then return to your scholars with fresh truth gathered and absorbed from pines and waters and deep singing winds, and you would find that they all sang of fountain-Love just as did Jesus Christ and all of pure God manifest in whatever form. You say that good men are "nearer to the heart of God than are woods and fields, rocks and waters." Such distinctions and measurements seem strange to me. Rocks and waters, etc., are words of God and so are men. We all flow from one fountain-Soul. All are expressions of one Love. God does not appear, and flow out, only from narrow chinks and round bored wells here and there in favored races and places, but He flows in grand undivided currents, shoreless and bound-less over creeds and forms and all kinds of civilizations and peoples and beasts, saturating all and fountainizing all.

John Muir (1838-1914)

*F*or of him, and through him, and to him, are all things: to whom be glory for ever.

Romans 11:36

*B*efore reaching...the goal of our pilgrimage, we were given the opportunity of contemplating many marvels. First there was Switzerland with its mountains whose summits were lost in the clouds, its graceful waterfalls gushing forth in a thousand different ways, its deep valleys literally covered with gigantic ferns and scarlet heather. Ah! Mother, how much good these beauties of nature, poured out in such profusion, did my soul. They raised it to heaven....There was, farther on, a huge lake gilded by the sun's rays, its calm waters blending their azure tints with the fires of the setting sun. All this presented to our enraptured gaze the most poetic and enchanting spectacle one could possibly imagine. And at the end of the vast horizon, we perceived mountains whose indistinct contours would have escaped us had not their snowy summits made visible by the sun not come to add one more charm to the beautiful lake which thrilled us so. When I saw all these beauties, profound thoughts came to life in my soul. I seemed to understand the grandeur of God and the marvels of heaven....I shall remember what my eyes have seen today. This thought will encourage me and I shall easily forget my own little interests, recalling the grandeur and power of God, this God whom I want to love alone.

Therese of Lisieux (1873-1897)

God's Providence controls the universe. It is present everywhere. Providence is the sovereign Logos of God, imprinting form on the unformed materiality of the world, making and fashioning all things. Matter could not have acquired an articulated structure were it not for the directing power of the Logos who is the Image, Intellect, Wisdom and Providence of God.

Anthony the Great (251-356)

Just as the sun shines simultaneously on the tall cedars and on each little flower as though it were alone on the earth, so our Lord is occupied with each soul as though there were no others like it. And just as in nature the seasons are arranged in such a way as to make the humblest daisy bloom on a set day, in the same way, everything works out for the good of each soul.

Therese of Lisieux (1873-1897)

If thy heart were right, then every creature would be a mirror of life and a book of holy doctrine. There is no creature so small and abject, but it reflects the goodness of God.

Thomas à Kempis (1380-1471)

And Moses said unto (Pharaoh),... I will spread abroad my hands unto the Lord, and the thunder shall cease... that thou mayest know how that the earth is the Lord's.

Exodus 9:29

The world in all its diversity and varying conditions is composed not only of rational and diviner natures, but of dumb animals, wild and tame beasts, of birds and of all the things which live in the waters.... Seeing there is so great a variety in the world, and so great a diversity among rational beings themselves, what cause ought to be assigned for the existence of the world? But God, by ineffable skill of His wisdom, transforming and restoring all things, recalls those very creatures which differed so much from each other in mental conformation to one agreement of labor and purpose, so that although they are under the influence of different motives, they nevertheless complete the fullness and perfection of one world, and the very variety of minds tends to one end of perfection.

And although the world is arranged into different kinds of offices and conditions, nevertheless the whole world ought to be regarded as some huge and immense animal, which is kept together by the power and reason of God as one soul. This is indicated in sacred scripture by the declaration of the prophet, "'Do not I fill heaven and earth,' saith the Lord"(Jeremiah 23:24), and again, "The heaven is my throne and the earth is my footstool" (Isaiah 66:1).

Origen (185-254)

*M*an, it is to be noted, has com-
munity with things inanimate and participates in the life of the unreasoning creatures, and shares in the mental processes
of those endowed with reason. For the
bond of union between man and inanimate things is the body and its composi-
tion out of the four elements; and the
bond between man and plants consists,
in addition to these things, of their powers of nourishment and growth and
seeding, that is, generation; and finally,
over and above these links, man is con-
nected with unreasoning animals by appetite, that is anger and desire, and sense
and impulsive movement...plus the five
physical senses....

Lastly, man's reason unites him to incorporeal and intelligent natures, for he
applies his reason and mind and judgment to everything and pursues after
virtues and eagerly follows after piety,
which is the crown of the virtues. And so
man is a microcosm.

John Damascene (675-749)

O Most High, Almighty, Good Lord God, to Thee belongs all praise, glory, honor and blessing!

Praised be my Lord God with all His creatures; and especially our brother the sun, who brings us the day, and who brings us the light; fair is he, and shining with a very great splendor; O Lord, to us he signifies Thee!

Praised be my Lord for our sister, the moon, and for the stars, the which He has set clear and lovely in the heavens.

Praised be my Lord for our brother the wind, and for air and cloud, calms and all weather, by the which Thou upholdest in life all creatures.

Praised be my Lord for our sister water, who is very serviceable unto us, and humble and precious and clean.

Praised be my Lord for our brother fire, through whom Thou givest us light in the darkness. And he is bright, and pleasant and very mighty and strong.

Praised be my Lord for our mother the earth, which doth sustain us and keep us and bringeth forth divers fruits, and flowers of many colors, and grass.

Praised be my Lord, for all those who pardon one another for His love's sake, and who endure, for Thou, O Most High, shalt give them a crown!

Praised be my Lord for our sister, the death of the body, from whom no man escapeth.

Woe to him who dieth in mortal sin! Blessed are they who are found walking by Thy most holy will, for the second death shall have no power to do them harm.

Praise ye, and bless ye the Lord, and give thanks unto Him, and serve Him with great humility.

Francis of Assisi (1182-1226)

*T*he heavens declare the glory of God; and the firmament his handiwork.

Psalm 19:1

*D*o not denigrate anything God has created. All creation is simple, plain and good. And God is present throughout his creation. Why do you never consider things beneath your notice? God's justice is to be found in every detail of what he has made. The human race alone is capable of injustice. Human beings alone are capable of disobeying God's laws, because they try to be wiser than God....

The rest of creation cries out against the evil and perversity of the human species. Other creatures fulfill the commandments of God; they honor his laws. And other creatures do not grumble and complain about those laws. But human beings rebel against those laws, defying them in word and action. And in doing so they inflict terrible cruelty on the rest of God's creation.

Hildegard of Bingen (1098-1179)

*M*y brothers, birds, you should praise your Creator very much and always love Him; He gave you feathers to clothe you, wings so that you could fly, and whatever else was necessary for you. God made you noble among His creatures, and He gave you a home in the purity of the air; though you neither sow nor reap, He nevertheless protects and governs you without any solicitude on your part.

Francis of Assisi (1182-1226)

*T*he divine art that is manifested in the structure of the world is not only to be seen in the sun, the moon and the stars; it operates also on earth on a reduced scale. The hand of the Lord has not neglected the bodies of the smallest animals—and still less their souls—because each one of them is seen to possess some feature that is personal to, for instance, the way it protects itself.

Nor has the hand of the Lord neglected the plants of the earth, each of which has some detail bearing the mark of the divine art, whether it be the roots, the leaves, the fruits or the variety of species. In the same way, in books written under the influence of divine inspiration, Providence imparts to the human race a wisdom that is more than human, sowing in each letter some saving truth in so far as that letter can convey it, marking out thus the path of wisdom. For once it has been granted that the Scriptures have God himself for their author, we must necessarily believe that the person who is asking questions of nature, and the person who is asking questions of the Scriptures, are bound to arrive at the same conclusions.

Origen (185-254)

*N*ow if I believe in God's Son and bear in mind that He became a man, all creatures will appear a hundred times more beautiful to me than before. Then I will properly appreciate the sun, the moon, the stars, trees, apples, pears, as I reflect that He is Lord over and the center of all things.

Martin Luther (1483-1546)

*Y*ou never enjoy the world aright, till the sea itself floweth in your veins, till you are clothed with the heavens, and crowned with the stars: and perceive yourself to be the sole heir of the whole world, and more than so, because men are in it who are every one sole heirs as well as you. Till you can sing and rejoice and delight in God, as misers do in gold, and kings in scepters, you never enjoy the world.

Till your spirit filleth the whole world, and the stars are your jewels; till you are as familiar with the ways of God in all ages as with your work and table; till you are intimately acquainted with that shady nothing out of which the world was made; till you love men so as to desire their happiness, with a thirst equal to the zeal of your own; till you delight in God for being good to all; you never enjoy the world.

Thomas Traherne (1637-1674)

*A*ll creatures are balanced upon the creative word of God, as if upon a bridge of diamond. Above them is the abyss of divine infinitude, while below them that of their own nothingness.

Philaret of Moscow (1652-1681)

In the beginning God created the heaven and the earth.

Genesis 1:1

He who blesseth himself in the earth shall bless himself in the God of truth; and he that sweareth in the earth shall swear by the God of truth, because the former troubles are forgotten.... For behold, I create new heavens and a new earth: and the former shall not be remembered.

Isaiah 65:16-17

For the creature that serveth thee, who art the Maker, increaseth his strength against the unrighteous for their punishment, and abateth his strength for the benefit of such as put their trust in thee. Therefore even then was it altered into all fashions, and was obedient to thy grace, that nourisheth all things, according to the desire of them that had need: That thy children, O Lord, whom thou lovest, might know that it is not the growing of fruits that nourisheth man: but that it is thy word which preserveth them that put their trust in thee.

Wisdom of Solomon 16:24-26

God's providence embraces the whole universe.... By contemplating the beauty and use of each thing, (one who has acquired the habit of detachment) is filled with love for the Creator. He surveys all visible things: the sky, the sun, moon, stars and clouds, rain, snow and hail ... thunder, lightning, the winds and breezes and the way they change, the seasons, the years...; the four-legged animals, the wild beasts and animals and reptiles, all the birds, the springs and rivers, the many varieties of plants and herbs, both wild and cultivated. He sees in all things the order, the equilibrium, the proportion, the beauty, the rhythm, the union, the harmony, the usefulness, the variety, the motion, the colors, the shapes, the reversion of things to their source, permanence in the midst of corruption. Contemplating thus all created realities, he is filled with wonder.

Peter of Damascus (ca. 1027-1107)

While observing that [the] gaze [of God] never leaves anyone, one may see that it takes such diligent care of each one as though it cared only for him, and for no other, and this to such a degree that one on whom it rests cannot even conceive that it takes care of any other. One will also see that it takes the same most diligent care of the least of creatures as of the greatest, and of the whole universe.

Nicholas of Cusa (1401-1464)

The heavens, as they revolve beneath His government, do so in quiet submission to Him. The day and the night run the course He has laid down for them, and neither of them interferes with the other. Sun, moon, and starry choirs roll on in harmony at His command, none swerving from its appointed orbit.

Clement of Rome (37-101)

You have then heaven and earth adorned, earth beautified, the sea peopled with its own creatures, the air filled with birds which scour in every direction. Studious listener, think of all these creations.... Think of all those which my narration has left out to avoid tediousness; recognize everywhere the wisdom of God; never cease to wonder, and through every creature, to glorify the Creator.

Basil the Great (329-379)

*T*o be properly expressed a thing must proceed from within, moved by its form: it must come, not in from without but out from within.

Meister Eckhart (1260-1327)

*A*ll things flow constantly from God, as water flows from a spring, and tend ever to return to Him as water tends ever to return to its level.

John Scotus Eriugena (810-877)

*T*he whole sensible world is like a book written by the finger of God, that is, created by the divine power, and individual creatures are like certain characters invented not by human judgment, but by divine choice to manifest and to signify in some way the invisible wisdom of God. But just as when unlettered people see an open book, they see the characters, but do not know the letters, so foolish people and natural human beings, who do not perceive the things of God, see the external appearances in these visible creatures, but do not understand their inner meaning. But those who are spiritual persons can judge all things insofar as they consider the beauty of the work externally, but grasp within them how much the wisdom of the Creator is to be admired.

Hugh of St. Victor (1096-1141)

All that I have ever seen teaches me to trust the Creator for all that I have not seen.

Ralph Waldo Emerson (1803-1882)

I seek acquaintance with nature — to know her moods and manners. Primitive nature is the most interesting to me. I take infinite pains to know all the phenomena of spring, for instance, thinking that I have here the entire poem, and then to my chagrin, I learn that it is but an imperfect copy that I possess and have read; that my ancestors have torn out many of the first leaves and grandest passages, and mutilated it in many places. I should not like to think that some demigod had come before me and picked out some of the best of the stars. I wish to know an entire heaven and an entire earth. All the great trees and beasts, fishes and fowls are gone. The streams, perchance, are somewhat shrunk.

Henry David Thoreau (1817-1862)

The visible world with its host of creatures is nothing else than the emanated Word which has disposed itself into qualities.

Jacob Boehme (1575-1624)

*T*he Maker-Logos joined everything in order that it be cosmos, as it is said, and inaccessible beauty; and nobody can create anything more brilliant or more magnificent.

Gregory Nazianzus (329-389)

*A*nd God said, Let the waters bring forth abundantly the moving creatures that hath life, and fowl that may fly above the earth in the open firmament of heaven. And God created great whales, and every living creature that moveth, which the waters brought forth abundantly, after their kind, and every winged fowl after his kind: and God saw that it was good. And God blessed them, saying, Be fruitful and multiply, and fill the waters in the seas, and let fowl multiply in the earth.

Genesis 1:20-22

*A*s for those who are far from God...God has made it possible for them to come near to the knowledge of him and his love for them through the medium of creatures. These he has produced, as the letters of the alphabet, so to speak, by his power and his wisdom, that is to say, by his Son and his Spirit. The whole thing of this ministry is performed by creatures for the benefit of those who are far from God.

Evagrius of Pontus (345-399)

*L*et us avoid staying in towns and villages. It is better for their inhabitants to come and visit us. Let us seek the wilderness and so draw after us the people who now shun us. For Scripture praises those who "leave the cities and dwell in the rocks, and are like the dove" (Jeremiah 48:28). John the Baptist lived in the wilderness and the population of entire towns came out to him. Men dressed in garments of silk hastened to see his leather girdle; those who lived in houses with gilded ceilings chose to endure hardships in the open air; and rather than sleep on beds adorned with jewels they preferred to lie on the sand. All this they endured, although it was contrary to their usual habits; for in their desire to see John the Baptist and in their wonder at his holiness they did not notice the hardships and discomfort. For holiness is held in higher honor than wealth; and the life of stillness wins greater fame than fortune. How many rich men were there at that time, proud of their glory, and yet today they are quite forgotten; whereas the miraculous life of this humble desert dweller is acclaimed until this day, and his memory is greatly revered by all. For the renown of holiness is eternal, and its intrinsic virtues proclaim its value.

Nilus of Ancyra (363-430)

hat is a charitable heart? It is a heart which is burning with a loving charity for the whole of creation, for men, for the birds, for the beasts.... He who has such a heart cannot see or call to mind a creature without his eyes being filled with tears by reason of the immense compassion which seizes his heart; a heart which is so softened and can no longer bear to hear or learn from others of any suffering, even the smallest pain, being inflicted upon any creature. This is why such a man never ceases to pray also for the animals, for the enemies of truth, and for those who do him evil, that they may be preserved and purified. He will pray even for the lizards and reptiles, moved by the infinite pity which reigns in the hearts of those who are becoming united with God.

Isaac the Syrian (7th century)

*W*hen…I prayed with my heart, everything around me seemed delightful and marvelous. The trees, the grass, the birds, the earth, the air, the light seemed to be telling me that they existed for man's sake, that they witnessed to the love of God for man, that everything proved the love of God for man, that all things prayed to God and sang His praise.

The Russian Pilgrim (19th century)

*A*nd God made the firmament, and divided the waters which were under the firmament from the waters which were above the firmament: and it was so. And God called the firmament Heaven. And the evening and the morning were the second day. And God said, Let the waters under the heaven be gathered together unto one place, and let the dry land appear: and it was so. And God called the dry land Earth; and the gathering together of the waters called he Seas: and God saw that it was good. And God said, Let the earth bring forth grass, the herb yielding seed, and the fruit tree yielding fruit after his kind, whose seed is in itself, upon the earth: and it was so. And the earth brought forth grass, and herb yielding seed after his kind, and the tree yielding fruit, whose seed was in itself, after his kind: and God saw that it was good. And the evening and the morning were the third day

Genesis 1:7-13

It helped me to look at fields, or water, or flowers. In these things I found a remembrance of the Creator. I mean that they awakened and recollected me and served as a book and reminded me of my ingratitude and sins.

Teresa of Avila (1515-1582)

When one is alone at night in the depths of these woods, the stillness is at once awful and sublime. Every leaf seems to speak. One gets close to nature, and the love of beauty grows as it cannot in the distractions of a camp. The sense of utter loneliness is heightened by the invisibility of bird or beast that dwells here.

John Muir (1838-1914)

Alone in distant woods or fields, in unpretending sproutlands or pastures tracked by rabbits, even in a bleak and, to most, cheerless day, like this, when a villager would be thinking of his inn, I come to myself. I once more feel myself grandly related and that cold and solitude are friends of mine. I suppose that this value, in my case, is equivalent to what others get by church-going and prayer. I come to my solitary woodland walk as the homesick go home.... I come out to these solitudes where the problems of existence are simplified. I get away a mile or two from the town into the stillness and solitude of nature, with rocks, trees, weeds, snow about me. I enter some glade in the woods, perchance, where a few weeds and dry leaves alone lift themselves above the surface of the snow and it is as if I had come to an open window.... It is as if I always met in those places some grand, serene, immortal, infinitely encouraging, though invisible, companion, and walked with him.

Henry David Thoreau (1817-1862)

"*T*he heavens declare the glory of God" not by speaking in voice audible to the sensible ears, but by manifesting to us through their own greatness, the power of the Creator, and when we remark on their beauty, we give glory to their Maker as the best of all Artificers.

John Damascene (675-749)

*L*earn in the creature to love the Creator, and in the work Him who made it. Let not that which was made by Him take hold of thee, so that thou lose Him by Whom thou also art thyself made.

Augustine of Hippo (354-430)

*D*eliver me, O God, from all idolatrous love of any creature. I know infinite numbers have been lost to you by loving those creatures for their own sake, which you permit, nay, even command, to love subordinately to you. Preserve me, I beseech you, from all such blind affection; be a guard to my desires, that they fix on no creature any farther than the love of it tends to build me up in the love of you.

John Wesley (1701-1791)

The divine nature has the property of penetrating all things without mixing with them and of being itself impenetrable by anything else.

John Damascene (675-749)

We worship the one God who fashioned the whole fabric with the instrument of elements, bodies, spirits, and by His Word commanded it, by the reason with which He ordered it…whence it came about that the Greeks also give the universe the name of "cosmos" ("order" or "harmony"). Invisible though He is, He is seen. Incomprehensible though He is, He is by grace revealed.

Tertullian (160-230)

From henceforth you will gaze at all times upon the spectacle of God's continual loving care for his handiwork. Your mind will be swallowed up in awestruck wonder, your senses will be silent, and you, O feeble man, will lie prostrate on your face in prayer, your tongue unable to speak, and your heart incapable of praying; for in wonder at these divine acts of the Creator even prayer becomes inactive. This is the inactivity which is superior to work, when a person is completely still in his senses and thoughts, and he lies continually prostrate before his Lord. Then even his bones in their silence will offer up praise to God during this apparent inactivity, as the prophet says, "All my bones shall say, O Lord, who is like unto thee?" (Psalm 35:10).

Isaac the Syrian (7th century)

We see the Creator by analogy. That is, by the greatness and the beauty of His creation.

John Scotus Eriugena (810-877)

My creatures are pilgrim travelers in this life, created to reach Me, their ultimate goal....

Who sees and experiences this revelation of My Name being glorified and praised in every created thing?

The soul who has shed her body and come to Me, her final goal, sees it clearly, and in her vision she knows the truth....

She sees this fully and truly in My holy ones, in this blessed spirit, in all other creatures, and even in the devils.

Catherine of Siena (1347-1380)

If a bird's nest chance to be before thee in the way in any tree, or on the ground, whether they be young ones, or eggs, and the dam sitting upon the young, or upon the eggs, thou shalt not take the dam with the young: But thou shalt in any wise let the dam go, and take the young to thee; that it may be well with thee, and that thou mayest prolong thy days.

Deuteronomy 22:6-7

We can gather that all the creatures of the world lead the mind of the contemplative and wise man to the eternal God. For these creatures are shadows, echoes and pictures ... and vestiges proposed to us and signs divinely given so that we can see God.

Bonaventure (1217-1274)

If I were to speak to the Emperor, I would, supplicating and persuading him, tell him for the love of God and me to make a special law that no man should take and kill sister larks, nor do them any harm. Likewise, that all the podestas of the towns, and the lords of castles and villages, should be bound every year on Christmas day to compel men to throw wheat and other grains outside the cities and castles, that our sister larks may have something to eat, and also the other birds, on a day of such solemnity. And ... whoever shall have an ox or an ass shall be bound to provide for them on that night the best of good fodder. Likewise on that day, all poor men should be satisfied by the rich with good food.

Francis of Assisi (1182-1226)

The very order, disposition, beauty, change, and motion of the world and of all visible things silently proclaim that it could only have been made by God, the ineffably and invisibly Great and the ineffably and invisibly Beautiful.

Augustine of Hippo (354-430)

The pay you receive from Christ is everything that you are and have in the natural order. For he gives and preserves your being and existence, the powers of the soul, and the powers of the body together with all external goods. The pay you receive from Christ is the whole universe; it is all his spiritual gifts.

Ignatius of Loyola (1491-1556)

And God spake unto Noah, and to his sons with him, saying, And I, behold, I establish my covenant with you, and with your seed after you; and with every living creature that is with you, of the fowl, of the cattle, and of every beast of the earth with you; from all that go out of the ark, to every beast of the earth. And I will establish my covenant with you, neither shall all flesh be cut off any more by the waters of a flood; neither shall there any more be a flood to destroy the earth. And God said, This is the token of the covenant which I make between me and you and every living creature that is with you, for perpetual generations: I do set my bow in the cloud, and it shall be for a token of a covenant between me and the earth.

Genesis 9:8-13

Grant us, Lord, to hope on His name, which is the basic principle of all creation, opening the eyes of our heart to know thee, who alone art highest of the highest.

Clement of Rome (37-101)

It would go a long way to caution and direct people in their use of the world, that they were better studied and known in the creation of it.

For how could man find the confidence to abuse it, while they should see the Great Creator stare them in the face, in all and every part thereof?

William Penn (1644-1718)

If the physician understands the anatomy of medicines and the anatomy of diseases, he will find that a concordance exists between the two....

The curative power of medicines often consists, not so much of the spirit that is hidden in them, as in the spirit in which they are taken. Faith will make them efficacious; doubt will destroy their virtues.... No man can rationally employ remedies without knowing their quality, and he cannot know the qualities of plants without being able to read their "signatures".... That which gives healing power to a medicine is its "spiritus" and it is only perceptible by the senses of the "spiritual" man. It therefore follows that spiritual perception is a teacher of medicines far preferable to all written books.

Paracelsus (1493-1541)

*A*nd the Lord God took the man, and put him into the garden of Eden to dress it and to keep it.

Genesis 2:15

*T*he goodness of God breaking forth into a desire to communicate good was the cause and the beginning of the creation.

William Law (1686-1761)

*W*hy was man created? In order that, by apprehending God's creatures, he might contemplate and glorify Him who created them for man's sake. The intellect responsive to God's love is an invisible blessing given by God to he whose life by its virtue commends itself to Him. A man is free (to fulfill this role) if he is not a slave to sensual pleasures, but through good judgment and self-restraint he masters the body and with true gratitude is satisfied with what God gives him, even though it is quite scanty.

Anthony the Great (251-356)

It appears that the entire world is like a single mirror, full of lights that stand in the presence of the divine Wisdom, shedding light like burning coals.

Bonaventure (1217-1274)

All creatures live in the hands of God. By our senses we can see only the action of the creature, but faith sees the Creator acting in all things. Faith sees that Jesus Christ lives in everything and works through all history to the end of time. The actions of created beings are veils which hide the profound mysteries of the workings of God.

Jean-Pierre de Caussade (1675-1751)

The creation of the whole creation is nothing else but a manifestation of the all-eternal, unsearchable God; all whatever he is in his eternal unbeginning generation and dominion, of that is also the creation, but not in the omnipotence and power, but like an apple which grows upon the tree, which is not the tree itself, but grows from the power of the tree. Even so all things are sprung forth out of the divine desire, and created into an essence, where in the beginning there was no such essence present, but only that same mystery of the eternal generation, in which there has been an eternal perfection.

Jacob Boehme (1575-1624)

I believe that God has created me together with all that exists, that He has given me, and still sustains, my body and soul, all my limbs and senses, my reason and all the faculties of my mind, together with food and clothing, house and home, family and property.... All this He does out of His pure fatherly and divine goodness and mercy, without any merit or worthiness on my part.

Martin Luther (1483-1546)

*T*hrough heaven and earth and sea, through wood and stone, through all creation visible and invisible, I offer veneration to the Creator and Master and Maker of all things. For the creation does not venerate the Maker directly and by itself, but it is through me that the heavens declare the glory of God, through me the moon worships God, through me the stars glorify Him, through me the waters and showers of rain, the dews and all creation, venerate God and give Him glory.

Leontios of Cyprus (556-634)

*U*ncreate, without beginning, immortal, infinite, eternal, im-material, good, creative, just, enlightening, immutable, passionless, uncircumscribed, immeasurable, unlimited, unseen, unthinkable, wanting in nothing, being His own rule and authority, all-ruling, life-giving, omnipotent, of infinite power, containing and main-taining the universe and making provision for all: all these and suchlike attributes the Deity possesses by nature, not having re-ceived them from elsewhere, but Himself imparting all good to His own creations according to the capacity of each.

John Damascene (675-749)

It was the Book of Nature, written by the finger of God, which I studied....Nature is the universal teacher. Whatever we cannot learn from the external appearance of nature, we can learn from her spirit. Both are one. Everything is taught by Nature to her disciple if he asks for information in the appropriate manner.

Paracelsus (1493-1541)

It is God who creates, effects, and preserves all things through His almighty power and right hand, as our creed confesses. For He dispatches no officials or angels when He creates or preserves something.... However, He Himself must be present and must take and preserve His creation both in its innermost and outermost aspects.

Martin Luther (1483-1546)

The earth mourneth and fadeth away.... The earth also is defiled under the inhabitants thereof; because they have transgressed the laws, changed the ordinance, broken the everlasting covenant. Therefore hath the curse devoured the earth, and they that dwell therein are desolate.

Isaiah 24:4-6

We cannot be excused when we have not at all considered God in His works. He does not at all leave Himself without witness here.... Let us then only open our eyes and we will have enough arguments for the grandeur of God, so that we may learn to honor Him as He deserves.

John Calvin (1509-1564)

T hou wilt find something greater
In the woods than in books.
The trees and rocks will teach thee
What thou canst not hear
From human teachers.

Bernard of Clairvaux (1090-1153)

O worship the Lord in the beauty of holiness: fear before him, all the earth. Say among the heathen that the Lord reigneth: the world also shall be established that it shall not be moved: he shall judge the people righteously. Let the heavens rejoice, and let the earth be glad; let the sea roar, and the fullness thereof. Let the field be joyful, and all that is therein: then shall all the trees of the wood rejoice.

Psalm 96:9-12

T hey may encourage us to imitate Him whose mercy is over all of His works. They may soften our hearts towards the meaner creatures, knowing that the Lord cares for them. It may enlarge our hearts towards those poor creatures to reflect that, as vile as they appear in our eyes, not one of them is forgotten in the sight of our Father which is in heaven....

Yea, let us habituate ourselves to look forward, beyond this present scene of bondage, to the happy time when they will be delivered therefrom into the liberty of the children of God.

John Wesley (1701-1791)

Consider the lilies of the field, how they grow; they toil not, neither do they spin: And yet I say unto you, that even Solomon in all his glory was not arrayed like one of these.

Matthew 6:28-29

I want creation to penetrate you with so much admiration that wherever you go, the least plant may bring you the clear remembrance of the Creator....

Scripture depicts to us the Supreme Artist, praising each one of His works; soon when His work is complete He will accord praise to the whole together....

A single plant, a blade of grass or one speck of dust is sufficient to occupy all your intelligence in beholding the art with which it has been made.

Basil the Great (329-379)

I was early convinced in my life that true religion consisted in an inward life, wherein the heart doth love and reverence God the Creator and learn to exercise true justice and goodness, not only toward all men, but also toward the brute creatures; that as the mind was moved on an inward principle to love God as an invisible, incomprehensible being, on the same principle it was moved to love him in all his manifestations in the visible world; and as by his breath the flame of life was kindled in all animal and sensitive creatures, to say we love God as unseen and at the same time exercise cruelty toward the least creature moving by his life, or by life derived from him, was a contradiction itself.

John Woolman (1720-1772)

*T*he stars awaken a certain reverence, because though always present, they are inaccessible; but all natural objects make a kindred impression, when the mind is open to their influence. Nature never wears a mean appearance. Neither does the wisest man extort her secret, and lose his curiosity by finding out all her perfection. Nature never became toy to a wise spirit. The flowers, the animals, the mountains, reflected the wisdom of his best hour, as much as they had delighted the simplicity of his childhood.

Ralph Waldo Emerson (1803-1882)

*T*hat God is the Creator of the world is accepted even by those very persons who in many ways speak against Him, and yet acknowledge Him, styling Him the Creator...while the very heathen learned it from the creation itself. For even creation reveals Him who formed it, and the very work made suggests Him who made it, and the world manifests Him who ordered it.

Irenaeus of Lyons (129-203)

For it is said that it is the wisdom of men to search out God's works, and to set their minds wholly upon them. And God has also ordained the world to be like a theater upon which to behold His goodness, righteousness, power and wisdom.

John Calvin (1509-1564)

If God were to withdraw his hand, this building (the creation) would collapse....The sun would not long return its position and shine in the heavens, no child would be born; no kernel, no blade of grass, nothing at all would grow on earth or reproduce itself if God did not work forever and ever.

Martin Luther (1483-1546)

The tree which moves some to tears of joy is in the eyes of others only a green thing which stands in the way.

William Blake (1757-1827)

For when he considers the universe, can anyone be so simple-minded as not to believe that the Divine is present in everything, pervading, embracing, and penetrating it? For all things depend upon Him Who is, and nothing can exist which does not have its being in Him Who is.

Gregory of Nyssa (330-395)

And Nature, the old nurse, took
The child upon her knee,
Saying: "Here is a story-book
Thy Father has written for thee."

"Come, wander with me," she said,
"Into regions yet untrod;
And read what is still unread
In the manuscripts of God."

Henry Wadsworth Longfellow
(1807-1882)

*N*othing in the universe that God created lacks fecundity. By contemplating what God has made, human beings should also recognize the way they ought to behave.

Hugh of St. Victor (1096-1141)

*G*od does not care only for the universe, He also cares for all of its parts.... If on entering a house, you should behold everything refined, well arranged and adorned, you would believe that a master presided over it, and that he was much better and above all those excellent things. So in this house of the world, when you look upon the heaven and the earth, its providence, its ordering, its law, believe that there is a Lord and Parent of the universe far more glorious than the stars themselves, and the parts of the whole world.

Minucius Felix (167-249)

*T*he firmament has the stars for its beauty, and dispassion has the virtues for its adornment. For by dispassion I mean nothing other than the Heaven of the mind within the heart, which regards the wiles of the demons as mere pranks. And so he is preeminently dispassionate who has made his flesh incorruptible, who has raised his mind above natures and has subdued all his senses to it, and who keeps his soul before the face of the Lord, ever reaching out to Him even beyond his strength.

John Climacus (579-649)

*I*n future times, "men will become poor because they will not have a love for trees...."

Nicephoros of Chios (1750-1821)

*H*ow great is the power of God! His mere will is creation; for God alone created, since He alone is truly God. By a bare wish His work is done, and the world's existence follows upon a single act of His will.

Clement of Alexandria (150-220)

I went to the woods because I wished to live deliberately, to front only the essential facts of life, and see if I could not learn what it had to teach, and not, when I came to die, discover that I had not lived.

Henry David Thoreau (1817-1862)

*G*od created everything, not only for our use, but also that we, seeing the great wealth of his creations, might be astonished at the might of the Creator and might understand that all this was created with wisdom and unutterable goodness, for the honor of man, who was to appear.

John Chrysostom (347-407)

In the beginning was the Word, and the Word was with God, and the Word was God. The same was in the beginning with God. All things were made by him; and without him was not any thing made that was made. In him was life and the life was the light of men.

John 1:1-4

The high and the low of all creation, God gives to humankind to use. If this privilege is misused, God's justice permits creation to punish humanity.

Hildegard of Bingen (1098-1179)

We do not know God in His essence. We know Him rather from the grandeur of His creation and from His providential care for all creatures. By this means, as if using a mirror, we attain insight into His infinite goodness, wisdom and power.

Maximus the Confessor (580-662)

There came to St. Anthony in the desert one of the educated men of that time and he said, "Father, how can you endure to live here, deprived as you are of all consolation from books?" Anthony answered, "My book, philosopher, is the nature of created things, and whenever I wish, I can read it in the works of God."

Evagrius of Pontus (345-399)

God is self-existent, enclosing all things and enclosed by none; within all things according to His goodness and power, and yet without all [things] in His proper nature.

Athanasius (297-373)

Since, then, God, Who is good and more than good, did not find satisfaction in self-contemplation, but in His exceeding goodness wished certain things to come into existence which would enjoy His benefits and share in His goodness, He brought all things out of nothing into being and created them, both what is invisible and what is visible. Yea, even man, who is a compound of the visible and the invisible. And it is by thought that He creates, and thought is the basis of the work, the Word filling it and the Spirit perfecting it.

John Damascene (675-749)

or the LORD thy God bringeth thee into a good land, a land of brooks of water, of fountains and depths that spring out of valleys and hills;

A land of wheat, and barley, and vines, and fig trees, and pomegranates; a land of oil olive, and honey;

A land wherein thou shalt eat bread without scarceness, thou shalt not lack any thing in it; a land whose stones are iron, and out of whose hills thou mayest dig brass.

When thou hast eaten and art full, then thou shalt bless the LORD thy God for the good land which he hath given thee.

Beware that thou forget not the LORD thy God, in not keeping his commandments, and his judgments, and his statutes, which I command thee this day:

Lest when thou hast eaten and art full, and hast built goodly houses, and dwelt therein;

And when thy herds and thy flocks multiply, and thy silver and thy gold is multiplied, and all that thou hast is multiplied;

Then thine heart be lifted up, and thou forget the LORD thy God....

Deuteronomy 8:7-14

*W*hen we hear that God made everything, we ought to understand nothing other than God is in all things — i.e., that He subsists as the essence of all things.

John Scotus Eriugena (810-877)

*C*reation is a bible whose letters and syllables are the particular aspects of all creatures and whose words are the more universal aspects of creation. Conversely, Scripture is like a cosmos constituted of heaven and earth and things in between; that is, the ethical, the natural, the theological dimension.

Maximus the Confessor (580-662)

*E*verything that lives is holy.
If the doors of perception were cleansed,
Everything would appear to man as it is: infinite.
He who sees the infinite in all things sees God....
What! It will be questioned.
When the sun rises, do you not see a round disk of fire,
Somewhat like a gold sovereign?
Oh, no, no! I see an innumerable company of the heavenly host crying,
"Holy, Holy, Holy, Lord God Almighty."

William Blake (1757-1827)

INDEX OF AUTHOR QUOTATIONS

BIOGRAPHICAL NOTES

JUDITH & MICHAEL OREN FITZGERALD have spent extended periods of time visiting traditional cultures and attending sacred ceremonies throughout the world. Judith Fitzgerald is a graduate of Indiana University. She is an artisan, calligrapher, and graphic designer, and has collaborated with her husband on several inspirational books. Michael Fitzgerald has taught Religious Traditions of the North American Indians in the Indiana University Continuing Studies Department. Three of Michael's books on American Indian spirituality are used in college and university classes. Michael holds a Doctor of Jurisprudence, cum laude, from Indiana University. They have an adult son, and live in Bloomington, Indiana.

The Fitzgerald family has deeded 342 acres located in both Santa Fe, New Mexico and Bloomington, Indiana into permanent conservation easements to prevent any future development

REV. DR. JOHN CHRYSSAVGIS was born in Australia. He received his degree in Theology from the University of Athens and completed his doctoral studies in Patristics at the University of Oxford. After several months in silent retreat on Mt. Athos, he served the Orthodox Church in Australia, co-founding St. Andrew's Theological College in Sydney. He has also taught as Professor of Theology at Holy Cross School of Theology.

He is the author of several books and numerous articles on the early Church Fathers and Orthodox Spirituality, including *In the Heart of the Desert: The Spirituality of the Desert Fathers and Mothers* (World Wisdom, 2002) and *Light Through Darkness* (Orbis Books, 2004). He has also published several books on Orthodox perspectives of the environment, including *Beyond the Shattered Image* (1999), and is the editor of the official volume on the ecological initiatives of the Ecumenical Patriarch, entitled: *Cosmic Grace, Humble Prayer* (Eerdmans, 2003).

What others have said about Michael Oren Fitzgerald

"Michael Fitzgerald has heard the poignant narratives of the American Indian people, and has lived among the Crow people for extended periods of time since 1970. He has studied American Indian religious traditions on the earth, among the people, in ceremonies and family gatherings. We thank Fitzgerald for his deep-seated appreciation, honor, and respect for American Indian culture, its religion, language, and lifeways."

—**Janine Pease Pretty On Top**, founding president of the Little Big Horn College, and recipient of the National Indian Educator of the Year Award

"He has a great sense of discernment in selecting editorial material which addresses directly the concerns of contemporary man."

—**Prof. Seyyed Hossein Nasr**, the George Washington University

"I greatly appreciate the recovery work that Fitzgerald is doing, work that makes available for the classroom and popular use texts that have been all but buried in libraries. Work such as Fitzgerald's is exactly the kind of work that needs to be promoted for a more complete understanding of early American Indian writings and oratory."

—**Prof. Stephen Brandon**, University of New Mexico

"My son, Michael Fitzgerald, has been a member of my family and the Crow tribe for over twenty years. Michael has helped to preserve the spiritual traditions of the Crow Sun Dance and he has helped to show us the wisdom of the old-timers."

—**Thomas Yellowtail**, Crow Medicine Man and Sun Dance Chief

Books Edited by Michael Oren Fitzgerald

Yellowtail, Crow Medicine Man and Sun Dance Chief, University of Oklahoma Press, 1991.

Light on the Indian World: The Essential Writings of Charles Eastman (Ohiyesa), World Wisdom, 2002.

Voice of the Guru: The 68th Jagadguru of Kanchipuram, World Wisdom (forthcoming 2006).

Books Edited by Judith Fitzgerald & Michael Oren Fitzgerald

Indian Spirit, World Wisdom, 2003.

Christian Spirit, World Wisdom, 2004.

The Spirit of Indian Women, World Wisdom (forthcoming 2006).

Free Christian e-Products

Daily Inspirational Quotations. Judith and Michael Oren Fitzgerald have also selected several additional Christian inspirational quotations that were not used in *The Sermon of All Creation* and designed and created many patterns of Christian e-stationery for use on the Internet. The quotations and e-stationery are combined to create "daily inspirational Christian quotations" that can be automatically sent to readers each day via e-mail at no charge. Interested readers should visit the "e-Products" section of the publisher's Internet site at:

www.worldwisdom.com

Other free e-Products

Judith Fitzgerald has also created Christian wallpaper, screen savers, e-cards, and e-stationery that are available for no cost at the same web site. New products are periodically added.

World Wisdom provides all of these products to readers at no cost. The publisher and the editors hope these products will also provide a source of daily inspiration.